A DORLING KINDERSLEY BOOK

Project Editor Patricia Grogan
Art Editor Peter Radcliffe
Managing Editor Jane Yorke
Senior Art Editor Marcus James
Production Lisa Moss

Published in Great Britain by
Dorling Kindersley Limited,
9 Henrietta Street, London WC2E 8PS

4 6 8 10 9 7 5

Copyright © 1998 Dorling Kindersley Limited, London

Photography (page 11, top right, Malayan flying frog)
copyright © Jerry Young

Visit us on the World Wide Web at
http://www.dk.com

A CIP catalogue record for this book is
available from the British Library.

ISBN 0-7513-5612-3

Colour reproduction by GRB, Italy
Printed in Belgium by Proost

Photography by Andy Crawford, Mike Dunning,
Neil Fletcher, Alan Hills, Dave King, Ray Moller,
Tracy Morgan, and Jerry Young.

Dorling Kindersley would like to thank
Almudena Díaz for DTP design, Mark Haygarth for
jacket design, Samantha Gray for editorial assistance,
Penny Lamprell for design assistance, Tom Worsley
for picture research, and Mrs G. Harwood for allowing
us to reproduce the photograph of her horse
Wychwood Dynascha.

You·Can·Draw

BRILLIANT CARTOONS

Grahame Corbett

Contents

DORLING KINDERSLEY
London • New York • Moscow • Sydney

Introduction

This book shows you how to improve your cartoon drawings quickly by following a few simple rules. First, consider the proportions of your chosen cartoon subject. Then draw some basic outline shapes, which exaggerate the features you want to emphasize. Finally, sketch in guidelines to help you position the details.

Exaggerating proportion

Before you start, study a photograph of the animal or person you want to draw. Look at the subject's pose, body proportions, and how the body parts align. Use this knowledge to decide which features to exaggerate to comic effect in your cartoon.

The real bear has a small head and pointed, fierce features.

The cartoon bear has a large, round body.

The head is drawn much bigger, and the facial features are enlarged and rounded to add to the friendly expression.

The bear's legs are almost half its total height.

The cartoon bear's legs are shorter and the feet are larger than a real bear's.

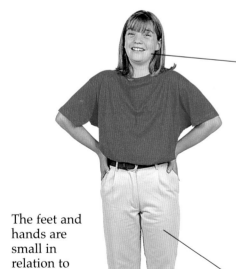

The height of this girl's head fits into her total height about seven times.

The head in this cartoon is twice as big as the girl's head in the photograph.

The hands look comical when they are made larger than in real life.

The smile is an ideal feature to exaggerate.

The feet and hands are small in relation to the rest of the body.

The top of the leg is approximately the half-way point on the girl's body.

The size of the girl's feet has been increased and the laces on her trainers exaggerated.

Using guideline shapes

The outline of your cartoon character is easier to draw if you divide it into a few basic shapes first.

Draw a detailed outline around the shapes.

Guidelines are drawn in blue to help you see them.

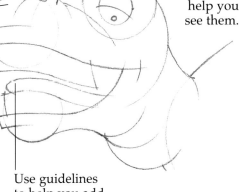

Using photographs

First, use photographs to look for features to exaggerate.

Here, the dinosaur's head and body are the obvious features to accentuate.

Drawing shapes

Start creating your cartoon character by sketching simple shapes to represent your subject's exaggerated proportions.

Sketch large circles and ovals to represent the head and body.

Draw simple lines to represent the legs.

Use guidelines to help you add the features.

Adding features

Finally, draw a more detailed outline around the simple shapes. Sketch in guidelines to position details and the features of your character.

Movement lines

You can bring your cartoon character to life by adding a few simple lines to indicate movement.

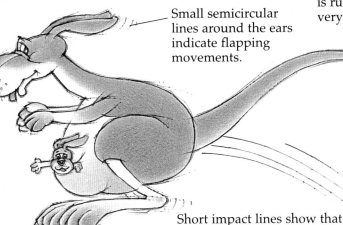

Small semicircular lines around the ears indicate flapping movements.

Straight whizz lines close together show the boy is running very quickly.

Light, dotted lines show the arms are moving up and down.

Multiple lines indicate fast-moving legs as the boy sprints along.

Short impact lines show that the kangaroo jumped from this point on the ground.

Long, curved, angled lines suggest a giant leap.

Drawing techniques

Use coloured pencils and felt-tip pens to draw your cartoons.

Use light-coloured pencils to draw your outline shapes and guidelines.

Rub out the guidelines you don't need, as you perfect your drawing.

Shade in your cartoons with solid colours.

Use a dark pencil or pen to draw a heavy outline around your finished cartoon.

Animal cartoons

Cartoon animals can be drawn in just a few simple steps. Whether you draw them from real life or from a photograph the rules are basically the same. Study the animal and emphasize its dominant features. Most importantly, add an expression that brings it to life and makes the cartoon funny.

Study the angle of the legs and tail before you sketch them in.

The chest and hindquarters form two circles.

Standing dog
Follow the steps on this page and transform this beagle into a cartoon. Exaggerate the tail, floppy ears, and big eyes.

1 Draw simple circle guidelines for the position of the body, head, and paws. Add lines for the legs and tail.

Draw a large eye to emphasize the dog's expression.

Rub out the guidelines you don't need.

Use a soft pencil to achieve a dark outline.

Make the body look stockier than it is in the photograph.

Leave a glint of white in the eye and nose.

A smile makes the dog look friendly.

2 Next, draw in the outline of your cartoon dog. Use guidelines to position the ear, nose, and mouth.

3 Finally, colour in the dog's coat markings and spend time developing the facial features.

Scratching dog
Now practise drawing your cartoon dog in a different pose, like this scratching dog. As before, start by drawing your basic guidelines. The shapes are the same, just placed differently.

Draw circles for the head, muzzle, and nose.

Add circles to the ends of the leg lines for paws.

Movement lines create a wagging tail effect.

Crossed eyes and raised eyebrows emphasize the dog's irritation.

Add lots of movement lines to animate the legs and paws.

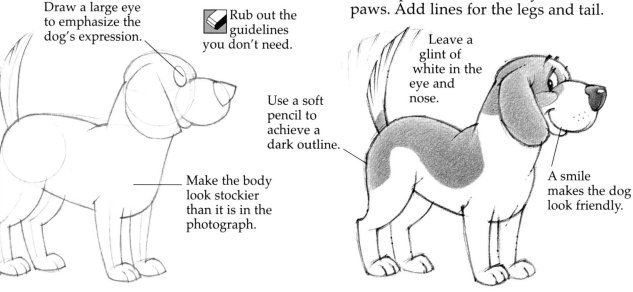

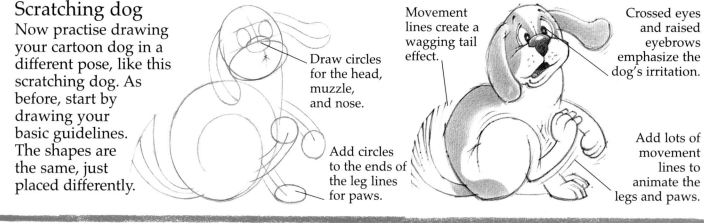

Prowling bear

Now try drawing this big, friendly bear. Study the photograph to get an idea of the most dominant features, which need to be emphasized in your cartoon version.

Draw two large circles for the body and shoulders.

Remember to make the eyes bigger to create a friendly face.

Add two smaller circles for the face and muzzle.

Draw lines for the legs and ovals for the paws.

1 Draw the guideline body shapes as shown above, making sure that the legs look shorter than in the photograph.

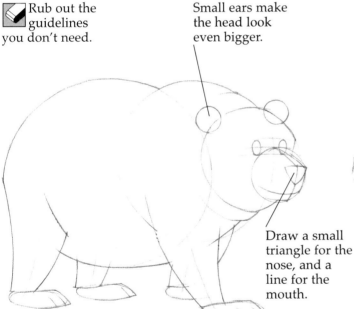

Rub out the guidelines you don't need.

Small ears make the head look even bigger.

Draw a small triangle for the nose, and a line for the mouth.

2 Draw in the bear's body outline. Use more guidelines to help you position the ears, eyes, nose, and mouth.

Use a soft, coloured pencil for the fur effect.

Raised eyebrows and a sideways glance give the bear character.

3 Now, draw the outline in dark pencil and shade in the fur. Colour the face in a lighter colour so that the features stand out.

Sitting bear

When you have mastered the bear cartoon above, try drawing it in a sitting position. This example has an additional prop, which helps to tell a story. The honeycomb and bees liven up the picture and add more character to the bear.

Draw the guidelines and shapes in their new positions.

The dripping honeycomb and bees show that the bear is hungry.

Soft, black outlines show the folds of flesh.

Draw the paws more like hands.

Animated animals

Animals move in many different ways. Whether they fly or leap, run or scurry, exaggerating their movements and body shapes adds humour to your cartoons. Look at the examples on these two pages, then have a go at drawing moving animals yourself.

Flying

This purposeful cartoon bird has a large beak and the straight movement lines emphasize its determination.

Draw semicircles for the basic shape of this bird's wings.

Movement lines animate the flapping wings.

Walking

These camel and lion cartoons reflect a proud arrogance in the way they walk. Both animals strut, hold their heads high, and gently flick their tails.

Add movement lines to show the hump is wobbling.

Use shapes to emphasize the knobbly knees and large hump.

A large semicircle for the mane takes up most of the body.

Short movement lines indicate the quick flicking of the tails.

Draw the feet at different angles.

The height of the lifted paw exaggerates the prancing motion.

The dragged-back ears give a sense of how fast the kangaroo is moving.

Bounding

The kangaroo's powerful legs and giant feet are exaggerated to show how it moves in leaps and bounds.

Long, sweeping lines show how far the kangaroo has jumped.

The body and muzzle are made up of ovals.

Short, fanned outlines show where the kangaroo bounced.

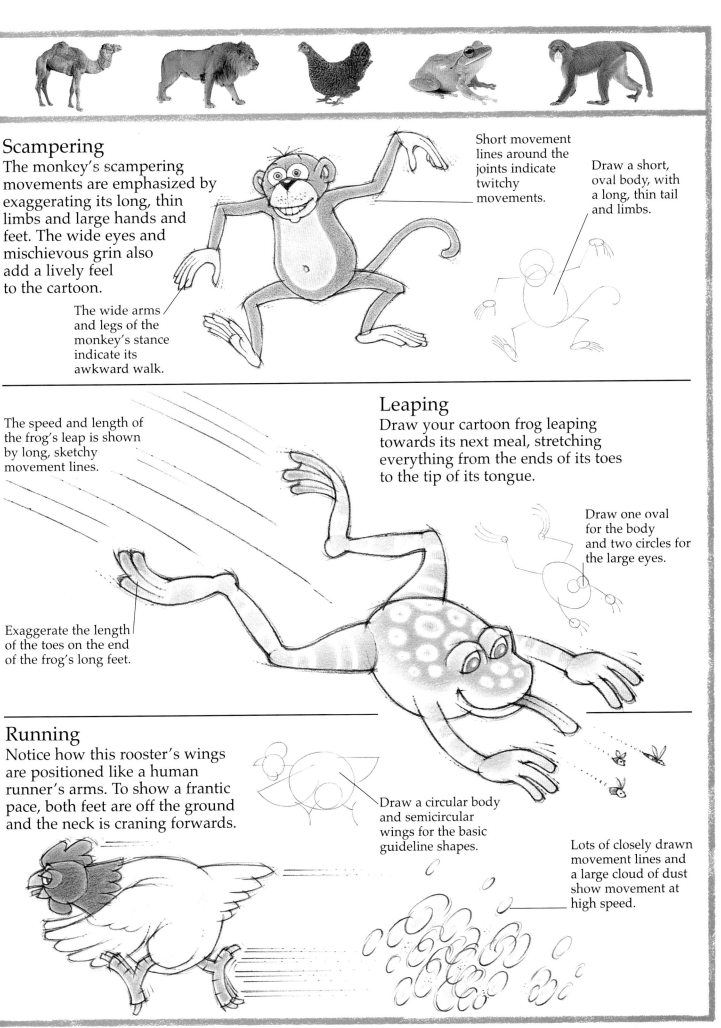

Scampering

The monkey's scampering movements are emphasized by exaggerating its long, thin limbs and large hands and feet. The wide eyes and mischievous grin also add a lively feel to the cartoon.

The wide arms and legs of the monkey's stance indicate its awkward walk.

Short movement lines around the joints indicate twitchy movements.

Draw a short, oval body, with a long, thin tail and limbs.

Leaping

Draw your cartoon frog leaping towards its next meal, stretching everything from the ends of its toes to the tip of its tongue.

The speed and length of the frog's leap is shown by long, sketchy movement lines.

Exaggerate the length of the toes on the end of the frog's long feet.

Draw one oval for the body and two circles for the large eyes.

Running

Notice how this rooster's wings are positioned like a human runner's arms. To show a frantic pace, both feet are off the ground and the neck is craning forwards.

Draw a circular body and semicircular wings for the basic guideline shapes.

Lots of closely drawn movement lines and a large cloud of dust show movement at high speed.

Monsters

Monsters make ideal subjects for cartoons because they have such distinctive features. This dinosaur, for example, has a very aggressive facial expression. The unusual body proportions make it easier to work out which features to exaggerate.

Vicious dinosaur

Follow the steps shown here and transform this roaring, *Tyrannosaurus Rex* into a monster cartoon.

Draw a large mouth with big circles for the muzzle.

Draw a large oval for the thigh muscle.

1 Draw large ovals for the body and a circle for the head. Add lines for the arms, legs, and large tail.

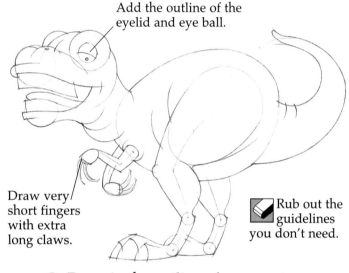

Add the outline of the eyelid and eye ball.

Draw very short fingers with extra long claws.

Rub out the guidelines you don't need.

2 Draw in the outline of your cartoon *Tyrannosaurus Rex*. Use guidelines to position the eye, nose, mouth, and fangs.

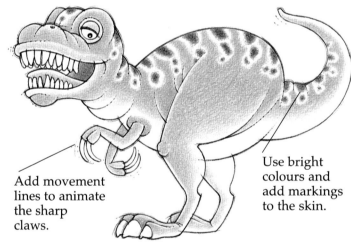

Add movement lines to animate the sharp claws.

Use bright colours and add markings to the skin.

3 Finally, colour in the *Tyrannosaurus Rex*, adding skin markings and claws. Spend time developing the ferocious facial expression.

Monster fish

Here you can learn how to transform this colourful fish into an underwater monster.

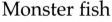

Use guidelines to position the fin shapes.

Sketch a large, oval body and a large, circular eye.

Draw line details on the fins, and finish in bright colours.

Add two large teeth for a monster effect.

Roaring dragon

Drawing fantasy cartoon characters allows you to let your imagination run riot. Here you can learn how to draw a dragon by combining the features in these photographs. Try drawing more monstrous combinations using other animals.

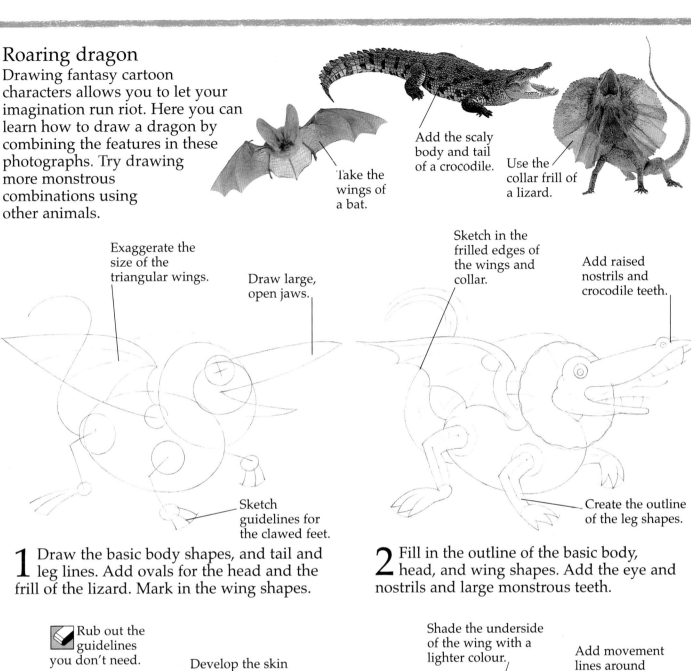

Take the wings of a bat.

Add the scaly body and tail of a crocodile.

Use the collar frill of a lizard.

Exaggerate the size of the triangular wings.

Draw large, open jaws.

Sketch guidelines for the clawed feet.

1 Draw the basic body shapes, and tail and leg lines. Add ovals for the head and the frill of the lizard. Mark in the wing shapes.

Sketch in the frilled edges of the wings and collar.

Add raised nostrils and crocodile teeth.

Create the outline of the leg shapes.

2 Fill in the outline of the basic body, head, and wing shapes. Add the eye and nostrils and large monstrous teeth.

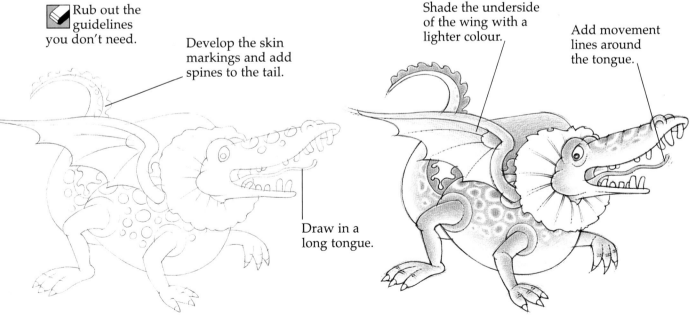

Rub out the guidelines you don't need.

Develop the skin markings and add spines to the tail.

Draw in a long tongue.

3 Spend time adding details such as claws to the toes. Draw markings all over the body, to give it a scaly look.

Shade the underside of the wing with a lighter colour.

Add movement lines around the tongue.

4 Finally, colour in your roaring dragon, using bright green or whatever colour you imagine a dragon might be.

Adding human characteristics to your animal cartoons gives your drawings a whole new lease of life. On these pages, you can learn how to combine the features of an animal with the postures and movements of a human, for some humorous results.

Use the body position of the girl.

Take the head of the rabbit.

Draw two long ovals for the rabbit's ears.

Draw a long, curved guideline through the middle of the body.

Draw large sausage shapes for the feet.

The hands and nose begin as small circles.

Walking rabbit

Use these photographs to study the body shapes of the human being and the rabbit. Practise drawing the rough shapes first.

1 Draw shapes and guidelines for the rabbit's body, head, ears, nose, hands, feet, and tail. Add lines for the human legs and arms.

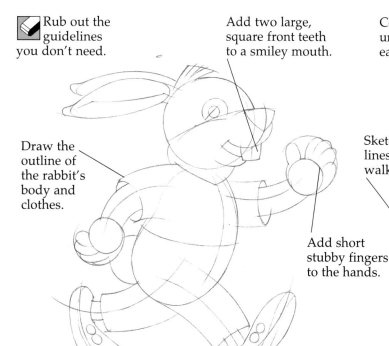

Rub out the guidelines you don't need.

Add two large, square front teeth to a smiley mouth.

Draw the outline of the rabbit's body and clothes.

Add short stubby fingers to the hands.

Colour the underside of the ears pink.

Leave a glint of white in the nose.

Sketch in movement lines to show a brisk walking pace.

2 Sketch the body outline, adding clothes and shoes for a more human look. Use guidelines to create a cheeky rabbit face.

3 Finally, colour in the rabbit, giving it brightly coloured clothes and shoes, some hair, and a glint in the eye.

Performing penguin

Here, you can learn how to draw a trumpet-playing penguin. Use the photographs to help you combine the shapes of a penguin and a trumpet player.

The trumpet is made up of three ovals.

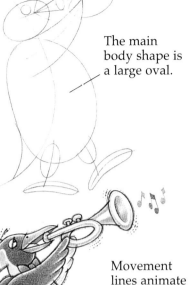

The main body shape is a large oval.

1 Draw the basic shapes of the penguin's body and head. Use guidelines to position the flippers like the trumpet player's arms.

Sketch in the large head and beak details.

Split the tail to make it look like a dinner jacket.

Complete the trumpet with a long cone shape.

2 Fill in the penguin outline, using the guidelines to position the details of the head and clothing.

Add a tuft of hair for a more human effect.

Movement lines animate the trumpet playing and foot tapping.

3 Finally, colour in your cartoon. Add movement lines and music notes around the trumpet, to bring your character to life.

Skating elephant

Now try drawing a skating elephant. Exaggerate the size and shape of the elephant, to make it look funny in the unbalanced position.

1 Start by drawing the rough, circular guideline shapes of the elephant's body, head, and legs, positioned as the skater is in the photograph.

Draw short lines for arms and legs.

Add shape to the elephant's trunk.

Develop the outline shape of the face and head.

2 Draw in the character outline, using guidelines to place the eye, ear, and trunk. Add clothes, helmet, skates, and knee and elbow pads.

Make the arms, legs, and body as chunky as possible.

3 Finally, colour in the elephant, giving it brightly coloured clothes and skates. Animate it with plenty of wobbly movement lines.

Movement lines emphasize the lack of balance.

Cartoon faces

Here, you can learn how to draw expressive, cartoon faces of people. Study the photographs on these pages, and make different expressions in the mirror, too. You can then work out which are the best features to exaggerate to create the expression you want.

Happy face

Follow the steps on this page and draw a happy cartoon face based on this photograph of a smiling boy.

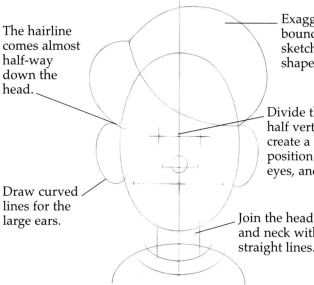

The hairline comes almost half-way down the head.

Exaggerate the bouncy hair by sketching curved shapes.

Divide the head in half vertically to create a guideline to position the nose, eyes, and mouth.

Draw curved lines for the large ears.

Join the head and neck with straight lines.

1 Start with an oval for the face, and a half oval for the shoulders. Draw guidelines to position the facial features.

Start breaking up the hair to make it look voluminous.

Sketch tiny circles for the eyes.

A circle helps create a button nose.

Draw a wide crescent shape for the mouth.

2 As you sketch in the outlines of the facial features, remember to exaggerate them!

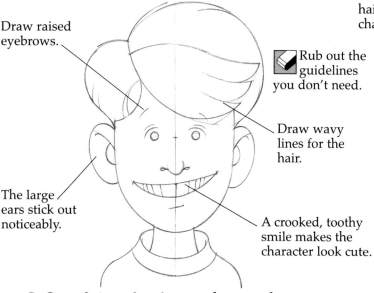

Draw raised eyebrows.

Rub out the guidelines you don't need.

Draw wavy lines for the hair.

The large ears stick out noticeably.

A crooked, toothy smile makes the character look cute.

3 Spend time developing the mouth, eyes, and ears. Draw semicircles around the eyes to make them look young and bright.

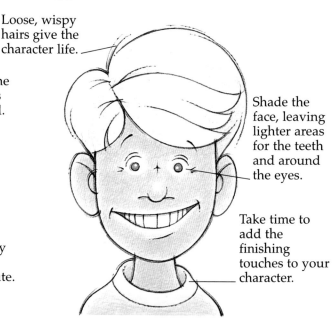

Loose, wispy hairs give the character life.

Shade the face, leaving lighter areas for the teeth and around the eyes.

Take time to add the finishing touches to your character.

4 Colour in your cartoon with bright coloured pencils. Leave a glint of white in the eyes to bring them alive.

Sad face

By lengthening all the features, you can make a face look sad.

The head is tilted slightly to one side.

Draw long, limp lines for the hair.

The chin is dropped down.

Sketch an elongated oval for the basic face shape.

Curve small eyes and eyebrows downwards.

Make the hair limp and wispy.

Use guidelines to help you position the facial features.

Make a down-turned curve for the mouth.

Angry face

An angry expression squashes the features together, narrowing the eyes and mouth.

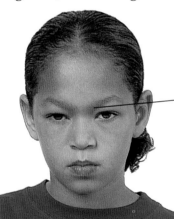

Draw basic shapes for the face and hair.

The eyes are narrowed and the eyebrows are angular.

Exaggerate the cheeks.

A middle parting emphasizes the features bunching up in the centre of the face.

Emphasize the V shape made by the eyebrows.

Use guidelines to sketch the eyes, nose, and mouth squashed up together.

Shade the face, leaving the eyes white and glaring.

Add lines around the eyes to emphasize the frown.

Surprised face

A surprised expression stretches the features apart and widens the eyes and mouth.

The chin is dropped and the nostrils are flared.

In a surprised expression the eyes are above the line of the ears.

Make the hair spring up in the air.

Sketch an oval shape for the face.

Draw a large circle for the mouth.

Lift the shoulders for added emphasis.

Raise the eyebrows.

Make the whites of the eyes very large.

Add two teeth only.

Cartoon people

You can take inspiration from anyone to draw a cartoon figure. The secret is to exaggerate body proportions and think of comical actions. These pages will teach you the basics. Once you have mastered the techniques, let your imagination run wild!

Laughing girl
Use this photograph of a laughing girl to help draw an exaggerated cartoon character.

Sketch in a curved guideline down the middle of the body to help you draw the tilted pose.

Exaggerate the tilt in the body by drawing one shoulder higher than the other.

1 Draw simple oval shapes for the head, body, hands, and feet. Add long lines for the legs.

Use guidelines to add the small eyes and nose.

Draw a large semicircle for the laughing mouth.

Start to add the outline of the clothes.

2 Sketch in the exaggerated body outline. Use guidelines to start building up the details of your cartoon.

Sketch in ovals for the large, comical hands.

The legs will look longer than they are in the photograph.

Make the fringe thick.

Draw flicked swinging ends to the hair.

Rub out the guidelines you don't need.

Sketch in the large fingers.

Draw trainer laces with overly large bows.

3 Complete the outline of the clothes and add a chunky belt.

Leave the large teeth white.

Sketch in guidelines on the large trainers.

Shade the T-shirt in a bright colour.

Ink in a dark outline around the cartoon.

4 Colour in your laughing cartoon girl. Add laughter lines around her eyes.

Running boy

Here, you can learn how to draw a character sprinting fast. Use the photograph to help you decide which features to exaggerate.

Draw the chest pushed out to make the character look as if he is making a real effort.

The limbs can be shortened for comic effect.

Dotty movement lines and vertical whizz lines add a feeling of speed.

Sketch a large circle for the head and a smaller circle for the ear.

Draw a curved vertical guideline down the middle of the body.

Add circles for the hands.

Draw in a large mop of hair.

Use guidelines to position the facial features in profile.

Make the arms angular.

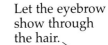Rub out the guidelines you don't need.

Let the eyebrow show through the hair.

Add large drops of sweat.

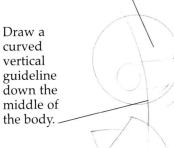

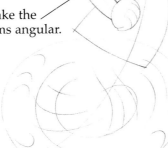

Draw curved lines for the feet positions.

1 Draw basic shapes and guidelines to help outline the figure. Sketch in a large oval for the running legs.

2 Sketch in the outlines of the clothes and face. Use guidelines to position the running leg lines.

3 Take time to draw in lines for the speedy legs. Finally, colour in your cartoon.

Hands and fingers

Cartoon hands are bulkier than real hands. Practise drawing hands and fingers doing lots of different things.

A simple circle forms the hand shape.

Draw short, stubby fingers, and circles for the nails.

Leave the fingernails white.

Palm

Draw chubby cartoon hands and fingers.

1 Draw a basic circle, larger semicircle, and lines joining the two.

2 Use the basic shapes as a guide to sketch in the outline of the fingers.

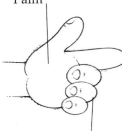

The fingers are elongated oval shapes.

Practise drawing hands holding or gripping objects.

3 Shade the hands to make them life-like. Keep a dark outline.

Cartoon characters

Cartoons often play on stereotypes. They build on certain features and make them even more noticeable. Here you can see how to turn a girl into a giant. On the next page you will find step-by-step instructions on how to draw a baby and an eccentric old character.

Tall girl
Use a photograph of a girl and a cat as a point of reference and inspiration to help you draw your tall cartoon girl.

Draw a guideline down the middle of the girl's face.

The oval for the girl's head is almost as large as the oval for her body.

Sketch very long lines for the girl's arms and legs.

1 Draw ovals for the girl's head, body, hands, and feet. Break down the cat's shape into a series of oval shapes, too.

Use guidelines to position the girl's facial features.

Make the T-shirt sleeves short to emphasize the girl's long arms.

2 Sketch in the outline of the girl's long arms and legs, large head and feet, and small body. Start adding details to the cat.

Add a toy mouse for comic effect.

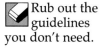 Rub out the guidelines you don't need.

Sketch a large, mischievous grin.

Give the cat character by making it scowl.

3 Complete the outlines of the girl, cat, and mouse. Add more details to build up the characters.

Draw raised eyebrows and leave a glint of white in the eyes.

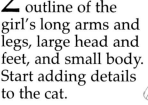

Short horizontal lines suggest the girl is patting the cat's head.

Large hands make the arms seem even longer.

4 Colour in your cartoon girl, cat, and mouse. Take time to add finishing touches to the facial features.

Laughing baby girl

Use a picture of a girl and a young baby as reference to help you draw a cute baby cartoon character.

Use the features of the girl's face and the sitting position of the baby to help you devise the cartoon character.

Draw a curved guideline down the centre of the body.

Sketch a triangle for the baby's fringe.

Add a frilly bonnet.

One large tooth makes the mouth look larger and the character younger.

Leave a glint of white in the eyes.

A large block makes her fingers look smaller.

Add the outline of the clothes around the guidelines.

Draw tiny circles for the gripping fingers.

1 Draw basic shapes for the different parts of the body and lines for the arms and legs.

2 Sketch in the outline shapes and start to build up details on the face and clothes.

3 Use bright colours for your cartoon baby. Add chunky toys to emphasize her tiny size.

Eccentric old man

Use photographs of an older man to turn a young boy into an eccentric-looking cartoon character.

Use the man's body and the boy's smiling face to help you create your cartoon.

Add glasses perched on the tip of the nose.

Add triangles for the hair on the balding head.

Add a knobbly walking stick.

Bundles of papers and books give a studious air.

Make the hair wild and wispy.

Add a baggy jumper, large shirt collar, and over-long trousers.

Use the guidelines to position the legs and arms.

Draw lines to show the trousers creasing around the ankles.

1 Draw a large oval for the body and smaller ovals for the face, hands, and feet.

2 Firm up the outline shapes and start adding more details to the character.

3 Use a dark pencil or pen to draw a heavy outline and colour in your cartoon.

Alien-Monster's
SLiMY
Activity Book

Illustrated by
Jonny
Duddle
and Aleksei
Bitskoff

Turn to pages 72 to 80
for the puzzle solutions.   YOUR ICKY STICKERS ARE AT THE BACK OF THE BOOK!

templar publishing

ALIEN-MONSTER I.D. CARDS

Meet some alien-monsters...

OFFICIAL
MONSTER
IDENTIFICATION

Name:
Tony Tripleye

Monster type:
Tripleye Vulgaris

Home: **Planet Haumea**

Skills: **spying on humans**

OFFICIAL
MONSTER
IDENTIFICATION

Name:
Speedy

Monster type:
Ripraptor

Home: **Planet Neptune**

Skills: **record-breaking runner**

OFFICIAL
MONSTER
IDENTIFICATION

Name:
Grace

Monster type:
Greed-o-gator Guts

Home: **Planet Grundle**

Skills: **eating at 100 miles per hou**

OFFICIAL
MONSTER
IDENTIFICATION

Name:
Donald

Monster type:
Dimdim

Home: **Mount Everest, Earth**

Skills: **hugging fast-moving lorries**

... then add a few of your own!

Stick in a photo or add a drawing

you

OFFICIAL
MONSTER
IDENTIFICATION

Name:
....

Monster type:
....

Home: ....

Skills: ....

OFFICIAL
MONSTER
IDENTIFICATION

Name:
....

Monster type:
....

Home: ....

Skills: ....

best mate

OFFICIAL
MONSTER
IDENTIFICATION

Name:
....

Monster type:
....

Home: ....

Skills: ....

family
member

Disgusting Monster Doodles

Colour in these ghastly guys...

"... then invent some new ones!

"Add my face, hair
and extra legs!"

"Give me a face
and wings."

"I need
my body!"

"I've got to
get a head!"

(Add monster doodles,
not monster doo-doos!!!)

CROSSWORD

DOWN:

1. A famous monster who likes to drink blood
2. Also known as the Abominable Snowman
4. Lots of these come out of monsters' noses
7. Also called droppings, or dung, alien-monsters have huge collections of this

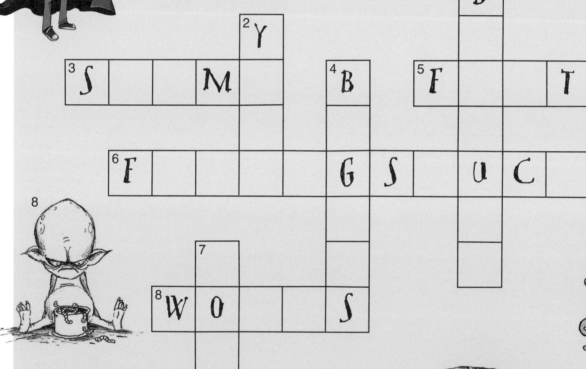

ACROSS:

3. A slimepud monster's favourite drink
5. Monsters power their stinky machines with these
6. A spacecraft that looks like a floating dinner plate
8. Aliens' favourite Earth-food (they live in the soil!)

Me and My Monster Shadow!

Match each monster to their shadow
by drawing a line linking them up.

Spot the Difference

Can you spot
ten differences between these
lesser-spotted pooters?

Greedy Grace loves to eat other monsters.

DO any of these little critters survive Grace's dinner-race?
Follow the trails to find out who escapes!

Fuzzball

Tracy
Tippytapod

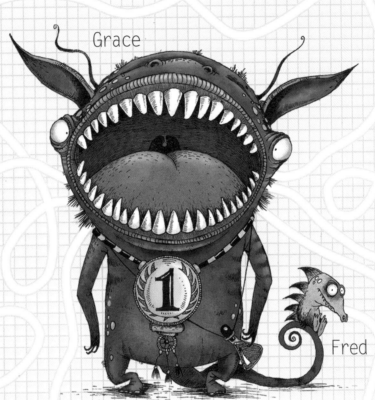

Grace

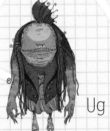

Ug

Mini Slimepud

Fred

Pooter grub

Inkfart

Venus F. Trap

Look Out!!!

These monsters have caught INVISIBILITY POX.
Cure them by drawing their heads,
bodies, arms and legs like so:

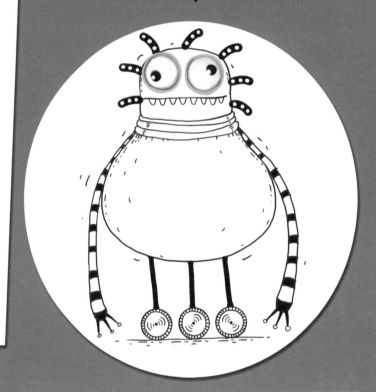

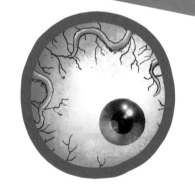

WORDSEARCH

Alien-monsters have lots of revolting body parts.
Can you find all 14 in this puzzle?

ARMS

EARS   EYES   TENTACLE

CLAWS    FUR   SPIKES

FEET   TEETH   TONGUE   WARTS

NOSE

TAIL

T	D	S	R	A	S	E	H	S	S
A	E	R	W	P	V	A	O	T	M
K	U	N	I	A	G	R	T	R	R
F	T	K	T	C	L	S	O	A	A
P	E	S	L	A	T	C	N	W	I
S	N	O	S	E	C	O	G	X	E
H	T	E	E	T	G	L	U	Y	G
R	X	F	A	K	R	S	E	P	X
K	L	I	A	T	G	S	L	Z	M
F	D	I	J	Z	V	O	B	D	A

LEGS

HOG-SPOTTING!

Howard Hoggernaut is looking
for his identical twin, Harry.
He is getting a bit confused,
as hoggernauts all look very similar.
Can you help him?

ALIEN-MONSTER TWINS

Can you match each set of twins and
spot which alien-monster is not one?

HALF AN ALIEN

Complete the dot-to-dot to draw
the other half of this alien, then colour him in!

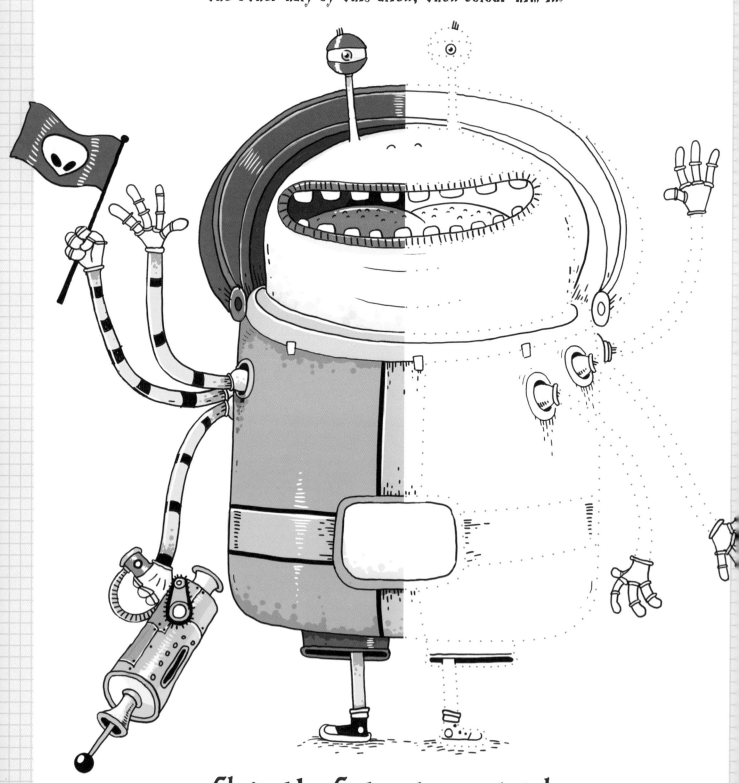

Elvis the Extra terrestrial

Brussel sprout

slime

stinky cheese

HUNGRY HENRY

This little monster is only happy when he can find some monster food to eat.

He loves slime, stinky cheese and Brussel sprouts!!! Nothing else will do.

Help Hungry Henry eat his way to the finish.
You can go up or down, left or right but not diagonally.
BUT REMEMBER: he only eats slime, stinky cheese
and Brussel sprouts.

START

Alien-Monster Shape Doodles

These might just look like funny shapes, but add eyes, hair, fur or fangs and you'll reveal aliens and monsters! Doodle, colour-in and don't forget to use your STICKERS.

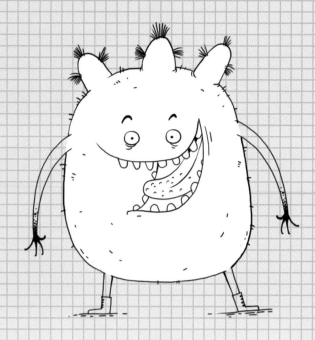

NAME: Lumpy-Bumpy

"I'm armless! Can you give me a tail or some tentacles?"

"I want a mouth that can scare all the other aliens!"

NAME:

NAME:

"My fur could be covered in fancy patterns!"

NAME:

NAME:

"I think I need a giant eye!"

NAME:

NAME:

Tasty Monster Meals

Monsters are very picky about food - only the finest slime and smelliest sludge will do. Can you invent a monster meal?

FUSTY FOOT SOUP
Boil for three months and it will taste just like chicken!

ALIVE EYES ON STICKS
Better than eye-scream, this is a tasty treat to serve at a party.

'THING' ON TOAST
'Thing' is even more delicious than Marmite™ when spread on bread.

SWAMP SMOOTHIE
Blended underwater monsters — crunchy and spicy!

Create your own monster meal:

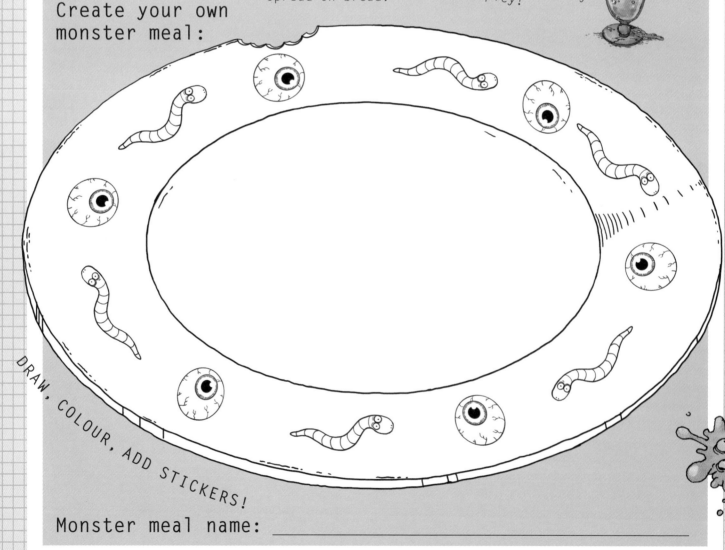

DRAW, COLOUR, ADD STICKERS!

Monster meal name: _____

Slimy Spawn Brew

Ghastly Ingredients:
- 70g of lime jelly
- 4 kiwi fruit
- 2 litres of lemonade

To make your slimy spawn brew:

1) With help from a grown-up, make the jelly according to the instructions, pour into shallow trays and put in the fridge to set.

2) Peel 4 kiwi fruit and cut into chunks, removing the white middle bit. Put into a blender with 750ml of lemonade and whizz for 30 seconds.

3) Cut the jelly into small cubes and place at the bottom of your jug, pour the kiwi mixture over the top and add the rest of the lemonade.

Monster-mouth Bites

Ghastly Ingredients:
- 3 red apples
- 1 bag of mini marshmallows (white)
- peanut butter (or chocolate spread)

To make your monster-mouth bites:

1) With help from a grown-up, slice your red apples into lip-sized chunks.

2) Take two apple chunks, stick together with peanut butter, keeping the red apple skin at the front and add marshmallow teeth.

3) Arrange on a plate into a smiley monster-mouth display.

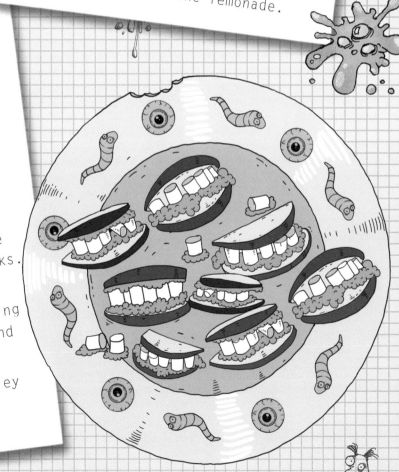

Monster Beauty
The smelly and dangerous bits...

Discover what are considered to be the greatest signs of beauty in the world of monsters!

TEETH
The best monster teeth are sharper than diamonds and can chomp through tin cans and car doors.

EARS
Gorgeous ears have poisonous spikes that can make victims blow up like a balloon.

NAILS
Monsters spend hours making sure their nails are as long, ragged and as smelly as possible.

WARTS
These can spit out poisonous pus, so don't get too close!

EYES
Goggly eyes are the most beautiful kind. If they look ready to pop out at any moment (or actually can be popped out) those are the best.

FEET
The best monster feet can be smelt from 100 miles away and are always growing a new crop of toe-cheese (a favourite food).

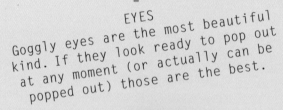

TONGUE
A tantalising tongue should be coated in farty-fungus-slugs that will make sure their owner always has knock-out bad breath.

SNOT
This must always be hanging out ready to be shot at enemies.

CAN YOU WORK OUT WHICH STICKERS GO HERE?

All alien-monsters love to collect spare parts so they can wear an extra flipper when swimming, a tentacle to get into those hard-to-reach places or a bat's eye for seeing in the dark!

SPARE PARTS

If you kept a jar of spare parts, what would you store in it?

DRAW, COLOUR AND ADD STICKERS!

ICKY STICKY ALIENS and MONSTERS

This curious-looking crew need some sticky help!
Can you find the perfect stickers to give back their missing body parts?

Gorgeous George has lost his monster ears and some of his icky toenails.
Use your stickers to give him back his monstrously good looks!

Monster Maze

Oh no, a human called Zak has got stuck in the monster maze!
Can you help him to find his way out, avoiding the
monsters that lurk around every corner?

HALF A MONSTER

Draw in the right side of this monster. You can copy
the left side or make up something totally new. It is up to you!

Derek Dentadontis

Monster FUN HOUSE!

Ten monsters live around this house. Can you find them all?

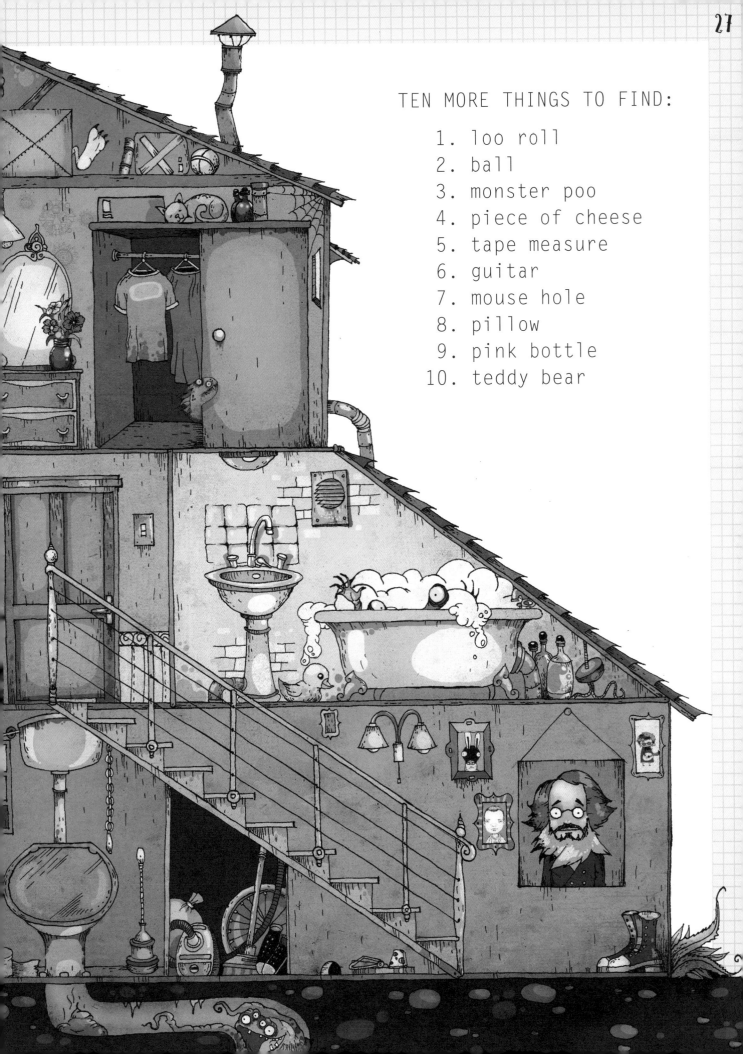

TEN MORE THINGS TO FIND:

1. loo roll
2. ball
3. monster poo
4. piece of cheese
5. tape measure
6. guitar
7. mouse hole
8. pillow
9. pink bottle
10. teddy bear

MY MONSTER STORY

Below is the beginning of your ghoulishly great monster tale. What will happen next? The STORY QUESTIONS and WORD IDEAS below and opposite will help you to finish this creepy adventure.

SPARE PARTS

On a normal Saturday, in a normal town, lived a very normal boy named Adam... or he WAS normal, until he visited the library.

Adam was looking for a book about monkeys when another one fell off the shelf called MONTY'S MARVELLOUS MONSTERS. As he picked it up, a note fell out:

IF YOU WANT TO MEET A MONSTER,

SAY THE TITLE OF THIS BOOK THREE TIMES.

Adam couldn't resist! As soon as he read the title for the third time...

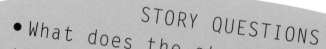

STORY QUESTIONS
- What does the strange book do next?
- What would a monster do in a library?
- Does Adam ever meet Monty himself?
- What happens to the monster and Adam at the end of the story?

WORD IDEAS

slime

swallow

chomp

book

hide

escape

tail

fly

warts

sneeze

catch

dinner

race

giant

How to Draw a Monster

You can make up all kinds of monsters once you know
what order you should draw each part in...

1. DRAW THE HEAD AND BODY

2. ADD THE ARMS AND LEGS

3. DRAW IN THE FACE

4. ADD OTHER DETAILS

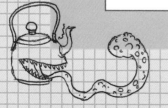

Level just high enough.

Now create your own monster!
We have got you started with step one —
the head and the body. Now you can make it
into any sort of monster you like by drawing
the next steps and colour in.

Don't forget to
name your monster!

Alien-Monster Puzzle

Look carefully, there are four pictures of each monster or alien.
Can you spot the odd one out?
Draw a circle around each one that is different.

We've done one to get you started!

This alien has no eye!

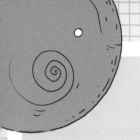

33

Decode the Alien Message

Scientists have discovered a message from an alien planet.
Can you rearrange some of the words that have become
scrambled to work out what it says?

Dear Zargle Neutron,

We hope your trip to ETRAH (_ _ _ _ _) is going well,
that your CROHET (_ _ _ _ _ _) has not malfunctioned
and that you are not eating too much Earth food.
All those rocks make you AATF (_ _ _ _)! Back here
on Neutron 7 we all miss you very much, but your
NIOMISS (_ _ _ _ _ _ _) to make contact with the
cleverest AMAILNS (_ _ _ _ _ _ _) on Planet Earth is
very important and we are ORUPO (_ _ _ _ _) of you.
Remember, when you meet them, not to say anything
about their strange SLIPPFER (_ _ _ _ _ _ _ _), and use
the polite form of the OIHOPLN (_ _ _ _ _ _ _) language.
VOLE (_ _ _ _),

Your Double-Parentoid

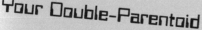

OUT OF THIS WORLD!

Make your own galactically great space scene

DRAW, COLOUR and use your STICKERS!

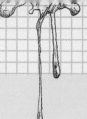

How to Draw an Alien

The trick to drawing great extraterrestrials is to create each part of them in the right order...

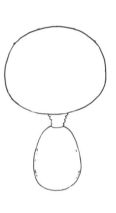

1. DRAW THE HEAD AND BODY

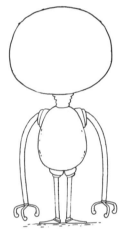

2. ADD THE ARMS AND LEGS

3. ADD ITS FACE AND HAIR

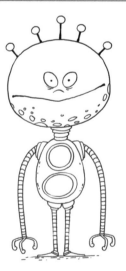

4. DRAW IN THE DETAILS

Now it's time to draw your own alien!
We've done step one for you, now follow
the other steps and colour in
YOUR OWN SPACE CREATURE!

ALIEN CALLED.......................... FROM THE PLANET ....

Moon Maze

Alien Pete lands his rocket on the Moon for a picnic – help him collect his friends from the centre of the maze and get to the picnic place. He must follow one continuous path, not going back over or crossing a previous route.

LANDING PAD

PICNIC PLACE

Star Man Dot-to-Dot

A star man has come to our galaxy.
Join the dot-to-dot stars to find out what he looks like!

STAR MAN CALLED

FROM THE PLANET

MIX-O-MATIC ALIENS AND MONSTERS

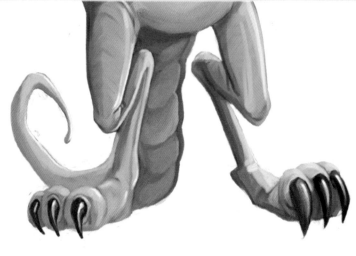

The Mix-o-Matic machine makes brand new alien-monster combinations.
Draw in the missing heads, bodies and legs to finish
these incredibly CREEPY CREATURES!

Where's my BEAR?

Donald Dimdim has lost his favourite pink teddy bear, called Fluffy. Can you help him to find it?

Draw a circle around Fluffy.

THE PLANETS TEST

To pass their flying saucer driving test,
alien-monster drivers must know the order of all the
planets in our solar system, from Mercury, the closest
to the Sun, to Neptune, the furthest away.
Can you find all the planets and the Sun,
hidden in this wordsearch?

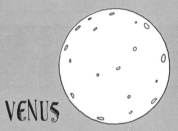

MERCURY

VENUS

EARTH

MARS

JUPITER

SATURN

PLANET COLOUR GUIDE

MERCURY – silver grey

VENUS – yellow

EARTH – blue and green

MARS – red

JUPITER – orange and white
(because it's always
covered in gas clouds)

SATURN – pale yellow

URANUS – bluey green

NEPTUNE – dark blue

PLUTO is not here because scientists
have decided it is not a planet.
They now call it a dwarf planet!

V	J	N	P	T	R	N	B	K	R	U	V	S	N	H
I	C	P	M	M	S	J	N	N	Z	E	R	E	F	X
X	Y	G	A	V	L	U	E	X	V	H	U	U	H	W
O	E	R	H	I	S	P	A	X	T	H	W	Y	H	Z
R	S	G	Q	M	T	I	J	R	L	K	O	N	G	J
L	V	U	V	U	M	T	A	F	N	V	L	L	Q	L
B	V	S	N	V	Y	E	Y	G	V	I	E	Z	A	A
N	T	E	K	A	C	R	Z	W	W	N	S	U	X	F
K	P	C	N	C	R	O	U	W	L	R	C	U	H	O
J	L	F	P	U	F	U	J	C	I	Y	J	L	U	R
B	Y	Q	H	A	S	A	T	U	R	N	W	S	V	M
M	Y	Z	S	G	Y	O	L	S	Q	E	G	A	B	L
O	K	O	J	W	N	J	Q	B	Z	T	M	K	H	Z
F	W	P	J	H	I	N	B	E	X	F	T	Y	H	J
T	V	O	C	A	T	S	D	U	F	A	E	A	L	T

URANUS   NEPTUNE

CREATE YOUR OWN SPACECRAFTS

Every alien dreams of making their own UFO
(unidentified flying object) so they can zoom around the galaxy!
First finish off some wild alien patterns on the rockets above.

You can customise the crafts below with windows,
booster rockets and whatever else you can dream up
to create the greatest super-fast spaceships.

Now doodle a totally
new spacecraft from scratch
in this space.

ADD STICKERS TOO!

MONSTER BEAUTY PARLOUR

Instead of going to the beauty parlour to get a suntan, monsters go there to get covered in incredible patterns.

Can you help to finish these ones off?

DRAW, COLOUR AND ADD STICKERS

add squares

add stripes

add spots

Fill this monster's tummy with shapes.
DRAW, COLOUR AND ADD STICKERS

Which Monster?

Look carefully at these monsters.
Can you see which one matches the silhouette exactly.

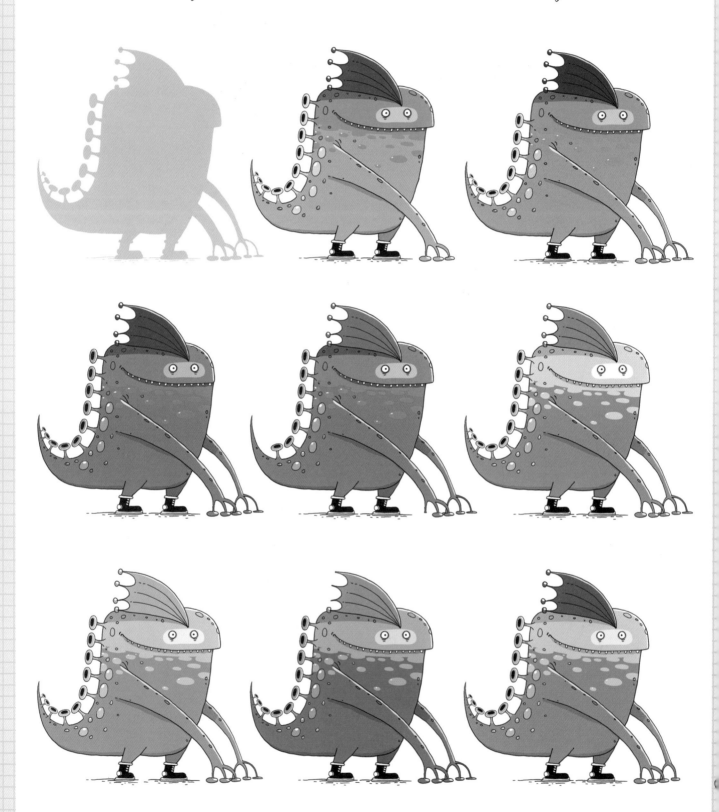

What is in a Name?

Hidden in each monster name are other words!
Can you use the letters to make 3 three-letter words,
3 four-letter words and even 1 five-letter word?

LOCH NESS MONSTER

FRANKENSTEIN

COUNT DRACULA

ABOMINABLE SNOWMAN

Monster Sticker Puzzle

There are lots of missing pieces from this jigsaw.
Use your stickers to complete the picture and you will
find out what this monster's favourite food is!

Alien-Monster Sudoku

Draw pictures of these four alien-monsters to complete the grid below.
Every row, every column and every four-square box in the grid
must include one picture of each alien-monster.
They must only appear ONCE in each row, column or box.

Alien Spacecraft

There is always lots happening
on an alien spacecraft.
Colour in to find: an umbrella,
an astronaut, five furry stowaways,
and six space cupcakes!

56

Which Alien?

Look carefully at these aliens.
Can you see which one matches the silhouette exactly?

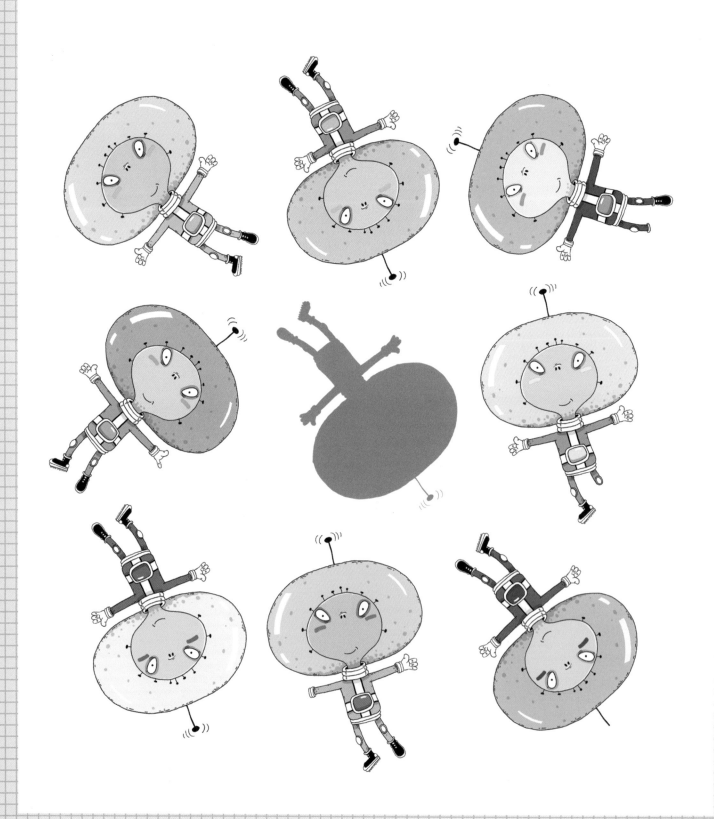

Words in Alien Words!

Hidden in each alien word are other words!
Can you use the letters to make three
three-letter words, three four-letter
words and one five-letter word?

ASTEROID

SPACE SHIP

STARMAN

Intergalactic Alien Treats

On long journeys into deep space, aliens love to eat food that reminds them of home. Now you can try out some of their unusual treats!

UFO Dip

Galactically Great Ingredients:
- 2 peppers of the same colour
- 1 large pot of hummus (or your favourite dip)
- Black olives or grapes

To make your UFO:

1) For your alien pilot's body, get a grown-up to slice off the top (stem end) of one pepper and scoop out the white ribs and seeds. Then add slices of olives or grapes to give him eyes, stuck on with hummus.

2) For the arms, again with help from a grown-up, slice the other pepper into strips.

3) Pick a flying saucer (or party bowl), put your dip into it and arrange your alien's body and arms. Serve with extra (terrestrial) veggies.

Star Fruit

Galactically Great Ingredients:
- 2 or 3 melons, one green, one pink and one orange
- A large bar of chocolate
- A star-shaped metal cookie cutter

To make your star fruit:

1) Get a grown-up to cut the melon into slices 1cm thick.

2) Using your cookie cutter, cut out star shapes from each melon slice.

3) Using a bowl of chocolate that a grown-up has melted, dip one half of each star into the chocolate, then stand it on a cocktail stick to harden. (You can even display your melon stars sticking out of half a grapefruit or melon!)

Alien-Monster Shapes

Use these colourful silhouettes to make up a whole mob of new alien-monsters!

DRAW, COLOUR AND ADD STICKERS

Find the Hidden Monster

Complete the picture below to reveal a monster surprise!
Use the dots when choosing what colour to use (so use yellow
where you see a yellow dot, blue where you see a blue one and so on).

Sticker Sudoku

Use your stickers to complete the grid below.
Every row, every column and every four-square box
in the grid must include one of the four pictures below.
They must only appear ONCE in each row, column or box.

OUTER SPACE LIMERICKS

A limerick is a short, funny sort of poem especially loved by aliens from outer space!

There was a young fartsquid from Mars,
Who loved to race friends round the stars.
One day he was top,
But went too fast to stop,
So now he's locked up behind bars!

Can you finish this limerick below using the words 'face', 'space' and 'Grace'?

A greedy young monster named _____ ,
Spent all day just stuffing her _____ .
With fungus and slime,
She had a fine time,
Now this monster's the fattest in _____ !

Try adding your own rhyming words
to finish off this limerick:

On Mercury lived a young _____,
Who loved nothing more than to _____,
Though slimy and _____,
He loved to try _____,
So now his friends call him the _____!

Now invent one of your own!

_____

_____

_____

_____

_____

ADD A PICTURE TOO

Monsters in Disguise
CROSSWORD

Monsters use disguises to get around the human world without being noticed. Spot the monster and name their disguise to solve this crossword!

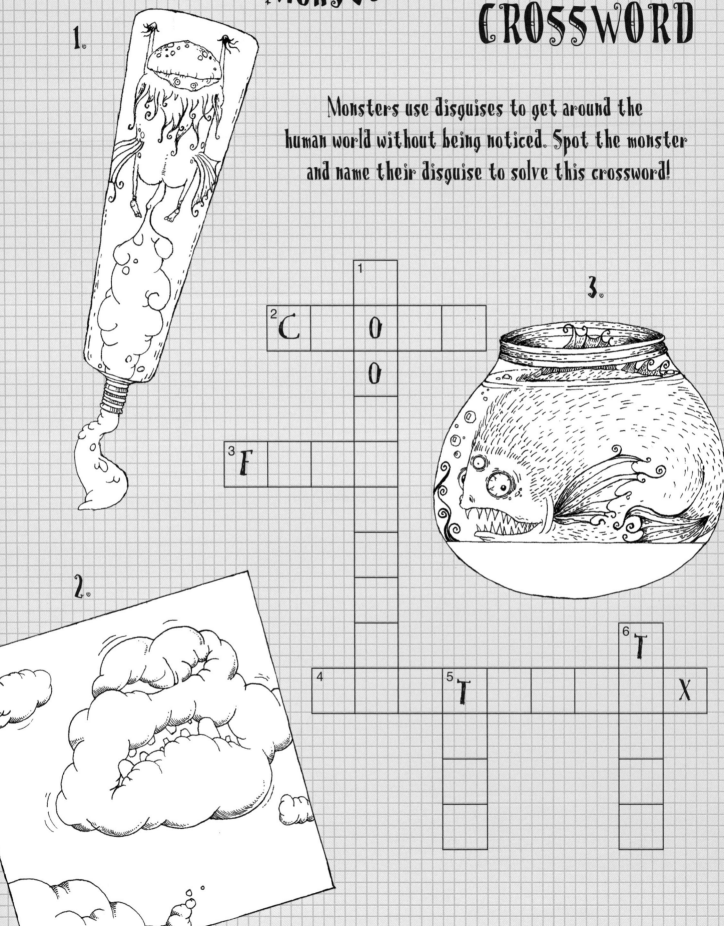

1.

2.

3.

1

²C O O

³F

⁶T

4   ⁵T   X

4.

5.

6.

NOW COLOUR IN THE MONSTERS!

Space Message

Sometimes aliens send messages using pictures instead of letters. Can you work out what this note says, using the translation guide below?

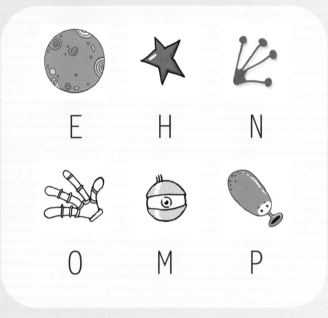

E   H   N

O   M   P

_____ _____ _____ _____ _____

WHO DUNNIT?

Someone has stolen Pinkie Batbean's whole house! The monster police have got three suspects.

Can you work out which monster is behind the crime, from Pinkie's clues?

SUSPECT 1:
TONY TRIPLEYE
• He is a lookout for a gang of monster burglars!

SUSPECT 2:
CAT-EYE CAZINSKY
• He's robbed three monster banks, using his tail to dig a tunnel under the safe!

SUSPECT 3:
ABOMINABLE ALBERT
• He uses his sharp teeth to escape by biting through his handcuffs.

CLUE 1: "It had sticky-out ears."

CLUE 2: "I saw green sparkling eyes towering over me!"

CLUE 3: "There were sharp, gnashing teeth!"

UNTANGLE TIME!

Some planets and spaceships
have got tangled up in the map below.
Can you tell how many of each there are?

NUMBER OF PLANETS:......   NUMBER OF SPACESHIPS:......

HOME SWEET HOME

Each of the alien-monsters wants to go home. Can you
draw a line to their home planet using their description?
(If you need planetary clues, go back to page 44!)

DONALD DIMDIM
lives on the highest
mountain on the same
planet as you.

HOWARD HOGGERNAUT lives
on a planet that's always
completely covered in
swirling gas clouds.

SPEEDY RIPRAPTOR'S
home is the furthest
planet from the Sun.

NEPTUNE

JUPITER

EARTH

TRACY TIPPYTAPOD lives on a red planet.

DEREK DENTADONTIS'S home has lots of rings.

FREDERIKA FARTSQUID lives on the nearest planet from the Sun.

We've done this one to get you started!

MARS

SATURN

MERCURY

72

ANSWERS

page 6
CROSSWORD

DOWN
1.DRACULA,
2.YETI, 4.BOGEYS,
7.POO

ACROSS
3.SLIME, 5.FARTS,
6.FLYING SAUCER,
8.WORMS

page 8
SPOT THE DIFFERENCE

page 7
ME AND MY MONSTER SHADOW!

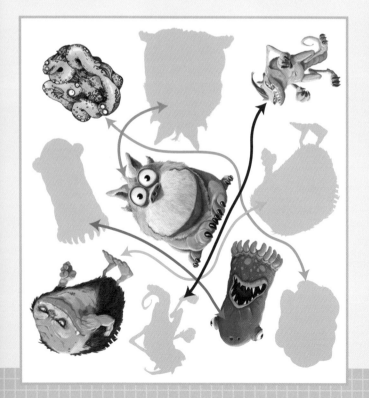

page 9
GREEDY GRACE

page 11
WORDSEARCH

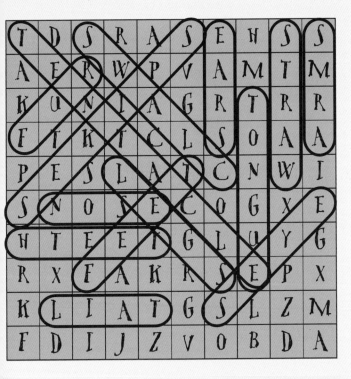

page 13
ALIEN-MONSTER TWINS

page 12
HOG-SPOTTING

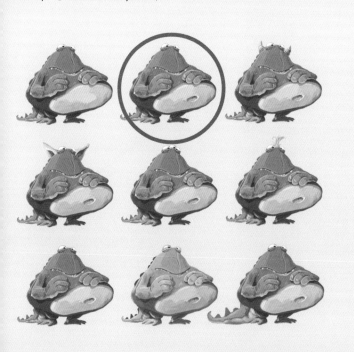

page 15
HUNGRY HENRY

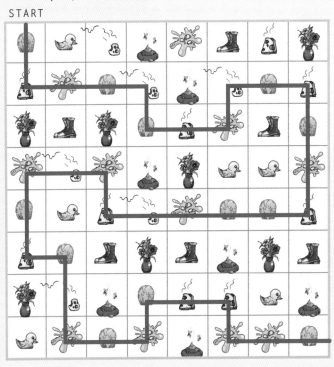

page 24 MONSTER MAZE

page 32
ALIEN-MONSTER PUZZLE

page 26-27
MONSTER HOUSE OF FUN

page 33
DECODE THE ALIEN MESSAGE

ETRAH – EARTH

CROHET – ROCKET

ARTF – FART

NIOMISS – MISSION

AMAILNS – ANIMALS

ORUPO – PROUD

SLIPPFER – FLIPPERS

DIHOPLN – DOLPHIN

VOLE – LOVE

page 38 MOON MAZE

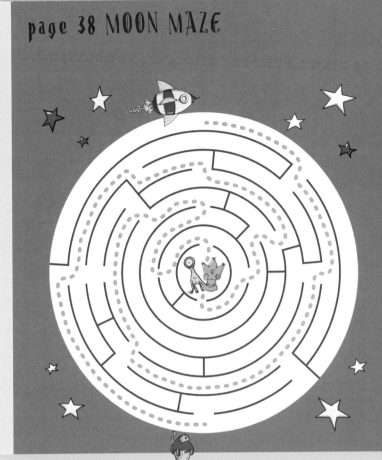

pages 42-43
Where's My BEAR?

pages 44-45
THE PLANETS
TEST

page 50
WHICH MONSTER?

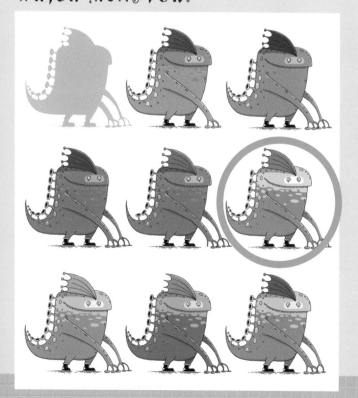

page 51
WHAT IS IN A NAME?

LOCH NESS MONSTER
hen, met, not,
mess, rest,
sent,
lemon.

FRANKENSTEIN
see, ran, net
star, nest,
fine,
snake.

COUNT DRACULA
out, and, old
card, toad,
aunt,
round.

ABOMINABLE
SNOWMAN
man, bob, moo,
snow, mine,
nine,
elbow.

PUZZLE NOTE:
these are just
some answers —
there are lots
more words you
can make up!

page 52
MONSTER STICKER PUZZLE

Favourite food : BEANS

page 53
ALIEN-MONSTER SUDOKU

pages 54-55
ALIEN SPACECRAFT

page 56

WHICH ALIEN?

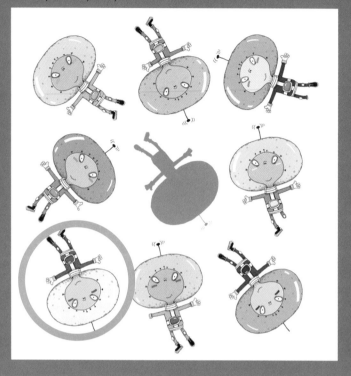

page 57

WORDS IN ALIEN WORDS!

ASTEROID
rod, sat, dot,
date, road,
idea,
tread.

SPACESHIP
pea, cap, ice
each, hiss,
chip,
chess.

STAR MAN
ant, tan, mat,
arms, mars,
mast,
smart.

PUZZLE NOTE:
these are just
some answers —
there are lots
more words you
can make up!

page 63

STICKER SUDOKU

page 66

MONSTERS IN
DISGUISE CROSSWORD

DOWN
1.toothpaste
5.tree 6.toast

ACROSS
2.cloud 3.fish
4.letterbox

page 68
WHO DUNNIT?

CAT-EYE CAZINSKY

page 67
SPACE MESSAGE

P H O N E

H O M E

page 69 UNTANGLE TIME!

Number of spaceships: **4**
Number of planets: **6**

page 70-71
HOME SWEET HOME

ONALD DIMDIM

HOWARD HOGGERNAUT

SPEEDY RIPRAPTOR

DEREK DENTADONTIS

TRACY TIPPYTAPOD

FREDERIKA FARTSQUID

NEPTUNE

JUPITER

EARTH

MARS

SATURN

MERCURY

1. Snotty
Nosiopolis, chief
bogey producer

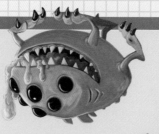

WHERE ARE THEY?

You have one last puzzle to solve!
Have you seen these alien-monsters in the book?
Look back through to spot which page they appear on.
(Answers below, no peeking!)

2. Undead Zed, the
king of the zombies

3. Harry the hairocoptor
gives lifts to other monsters

4. A Blurg,
the most ugly
of all aliens

A TEMPLAR BOOK

First published in the UK in 2014 by Templar Publishing,
an imprint of the Templar Company Limited,
Deepdene Lodge, Deepdene Avenue, Dorking, Surrey, RH5 4AT, UK
www.templarco.co.uk

Copyright © 2014 by The Templar Company Limited

Recommended for ages 4+

1 3 5 7 9 10 8 6 4 2
1213 007

All rights reserved

Designed by janie louise hunt • Written and edited by Libby Hamilton

ISBN 978-1-84877-918-1

Printed in Malaysia

WHERE ARE THEY? 1. PAGE 43 2. PAGE 3 3. PAGE 8 4. PAGE 69